Do You Even Know? How Much I Miss You?

Kyu? Hai na special?, Volume 4

Mrigendra Bharti

Published by Sellbrochure Vymish Entertainment, 2024.

DO YOU EVEN KNOW? HOW MUCH I MISS YOU?

First edition. September 12, 2024.

Copyright © 2024 Mrigendra Bharti.

ISBN: 979-8227754813

Written by Mrigendra Bharti.

Table of Contents

For Her

To Sugar of my Sweets,

This book stands as a testament to you, a canvas where every word and every poem is imbued with the hues of my deepest affection. As you turn these pages, know that each line reflects how uniquely you inspire me. This collection is more than just poetry—it is my heartfelt declaration that you are unlike anyone else in my life.

In a world overflowing with ordinary expressions, I sought to offer you something truly extraordinary. I wanted to create a tribute as distinctive and beautiful as you are. Each poem is a whisper of my admiration, a celebration of the way you illuminate my world. Your presence is a rare and wonderful gift, and I aimed to capture that exceptional quality in these verses.

Your smile, your laughter, and the way you brighten even the dullest of days are the true muses behind this book. This journey through my feelings is expressed in ways I hope will make your heart flutter and your cheeks blush. You deserve a love as special as you are, and this collection is my attempt to offer just that.

As you read these poems, remember they are crafted with you in mind. They represent my deep appreciation and the profound impact you have on my life. This book is for you and you alone—my muse, my inspiration, my everything.

With all my love,

Mrigendra Bharti

Preface

In a world where emotions often go unspoken and feelings remain hidden, this book seeks to give voice to the silent yearnings of one-sided love. "Do You Even Know? How Much I Miss You?" is a collection of poems that captures the essence of longing and the deep, unexpressed emotions that come with loving someone from afar.

Each poem in this book is a reflection of the moments I spend thinking about you, even though you may not be aware of it. The poems are accompanied by brief explanations that offer a glimpse into the heart of someone who constantly reminisces, cherishes memories, and grapples with the silence that comes from unreciprocated affection.

As you turn these pages, you will find a journey through the quiet battles of one-sided love, where every thought, every daydream, and every unanswered message becomes a testament to a love that is both enduring and unspoken.

This book is my way of reaching out, even if only through words, to let you know just how deeply you are remembered and cherished. Whether you find solace in these verses or simply recognize the reflections of your own experiences, I hope you find this collection as meaningful to you as it has been to me in writing it.

Series Overview: Kyu? Hai na Special?

In a world where expressions of love often blend into the mundane, Kyu? Hai na Special? stands as a beacon of originality. This series, crafted with deep admiration and affection, explores a distinctive approach to celebrating someone truly exceptional. The title itself poses a question that invites curiosity—why is this approach special? The answer lies in the way each book is meticulously designed to honor a singular muse, whose essence and charm transcend the ordinary. Every poem and every word within these pages are dedicated to a princess-like figure, embodying grace and elegance that inspire each verse.

As you journey through this series, you will discover that each book is not just a collection of poems but a tribute to a unique individual whose impact is both profound and unparalleled. The distinctive approach captured in these works reflects a heartfelt dedication, celebrating a presence that turns the everyday into something extraordinary.

Kyu? Hai na Special? is more than just a title—it is a declaration of the exceptional nature of the muse behind these verses and an invitation to experience love expressed in a truly remarkable way.

Acknowledgment

In the quiet moments of reflection, I find myself overwhelmed with gratitude for the inspiration behind this book. This collection of poems is dedicated to a remarkable presence, a person whose essence has infused every word and sentiment within these pages.

To the one whose grace and charm have transformed the ordinary into the extraordinary, I extend my deepest thanks. Your influence has shaped these verses and turned them into a celebration of the unique and the beautiful. It is your spirit that has guided each line, and your elegance that has inspired each thought.

Though your name remains unspoken, your impact is profoundly felt in every stanza. This book stands as a testament to the admiration and affection you have sparked. Your presence has been the muse that turned fleeting moments into lasting expressions of love.

Thank you for being a beacon of inspiration. This work is a tribute to you and a reflection of the exceptional qualities that make you truly special.

With heartfelt appreciation,
Mrigendra Bharti

About Sellbrochure IPDP

Sellbrochure Vymish Entertainment, recognized as India's largest book publishing company, has made significant strides in ensuring its extensive collection of books reaches audiences across the global market. This rapid expansion is a testament to the company's dedication to disseminating knowledge and literature far beyond national borders. Central to its success is its affiliation with InkWhirl Media Networks, a reputable entity in the media and publication industry known for its innovative and strategic approaches. Within this network, InkWhirl Publication LLC operates as a vital division, further enhancing the company's capabilities and reach in the international market. The visionary behind this enterprise is Mrigendra Bharti, the founder of Sellbrochure Vymish Entertainment. His foresight and passion for the literary world have been instrumental in steering the company towards remarkable growth and recognition. Under his leadership, Sellbrochure Vymish Entertainment has not only expanded its catalog but also established a strong presence in both domestic and international markets. Mrigendra Bharti's commitment to excellence and innovation has been a driving force in the company's journey, ensuring that it stays ahead of industry trends and meets the evolving needs of readers worldwide.

Sellbrochure Vymish Entertainment operates under the robust support of its parental organization, Mrigendra Bharti Group

InfoTech. This affiliation provides the necessary resources and strategic guidance, enabling the publishing company to undertake ambitious projects and explore new markets. Mrigendra Bharti Group InfoTech's extensive experience in technology and information services has been a valuable asset, allowing Sellbrochure Vymish Entertainment to integrate advanced digital solutions in its operations, thereby enhancing its distribution capabilities and reader engagement.

Through relentless efforts and a commitment to quality, Sellbrochure Vymish Entertainment continues to break barriers and expand the reach of Indian literature globally. The company's diverse portfolio includes a wide range of genres, catering to different age groups and interests, thereby fostering a rich and inclusive reading culture. As it continues to innovate and grow, Sellbrochure Vymish Entertainment remains dedicated to its mission of making literature accessible to all, contributing significantly to the global literary landscape.

Connect With Mrigendra,
Thank you very much for choosing this book.
You can also connect with me on Instagram,
https://www.instagram.com/i_mrigendrabharti.official
With Love,
Mrigendra Bharti

Introduction

Welcome to "Do You Even Know? How Much I Miss You?" — a journey through the unspoken depths of one-sided love, expressed through poetry. This book is a heartfelt exploration of the emotions that linger in the silence between us, revealing the profound impact of a love that remains unacknowledged.

In these pages, you will find a series of poems that articulate the essence of longing, the ache of separation, and the quiet yearning that accompanies unrequited affection. Each poem is paired with a brief explanation that offers insight into the thoughts and feelings behind the words, providing a deeper understanding of the emotional landscape that defines this collection.

This book is not just a compilation of verses but a window into the inner world of someone who constantly remembers and cherishes moments that may never be shared. It reflects on the daily rituals of love, from the hopeful anticipation of a message to the melancholic reflections of what might have been.

As you read, you may find echoes of your own experiences and emotions in these lines. The poems capture a universal truth — that love, whether spoken or silent, carries with it an undeniable weight and significance. My hope is that these verses offer solace and understanding, and that they resonate with anyone who has ever loved deeply from a distance.

Thank you for joining me on this journey. May these poems touch your heart as they have touched mine.

So let's start......

In Every Thought, You're There

Every night, when I close my eyes, you're the one I think of. Even though you're far away, your presence fills every corner of my mind. There's an emptiness because you're not here, but remembering you brings a strange kind of peace. No matter how distant we've become, you're still within my heart, and every moment, I find myself thinking only of you.

—

When the night falls, and all is still,
In my dreams, you linger still.
Though you're far, I feel you near,
Your memory whispers in my ear.
I wake to thoughts of you again,
Your absence like a soft refrain.
No matter where you choose to be,
In every thought, you're here with me.

In Every Thought, You're There

Every day I find myself thinking about you, even though you may not speak to me or want to stay connected. I look at your profile, read our old chats, and wonder if things could have been different. Sometimes I want to message you, but I hold back, fearing no reply. Still, before I sleep, you're the last thought in my mind, and every tear I shed carries your memory. I wake up with the same ache, but even in this silence, you're always with me.

—-

Each night I scroll through memories past,
Your words, your smile, they never last.
I type a message, then erase,
Afraid to send, afraid of space.
Your profile's all I see at night,
In those moments, you feel so right.
But silence fills the empty air,
And I'm left wondering if you care.
I dream of days we used to talk,
When every word made my heart stop.
Now tears are all that touch my face,
Yet in my thoughts, you still have place.
I check my phone, I hope, I sigh,
But all I do is close my eyes.
No message sent, no voice I hear,

Still, you remain so painfully near.
Though you're distant, far away,
In my heart, you always stay.
And every night before I sleep,
It's thoughts of you I always keep.

A Silent Message

"Every time I pick up my phone, I want to text you. My fingers hover over the keyboard, but I stop myself. I know you might not respond, but it doesn't change the fact that I want to reach out. Instead, I stare at our old messages and wonder what went wrong. I wish things were different, but for now, I send silent messages through my thoughts, hoping somehow they'll reach you."

—-

I draft a text, then let it go,
Hoping you'll feel what I can't show.
The words I wish I could convey,
Are left unsent, just fade away.
I stare at chats from days gone by,
And wonder if you ever try
To think of me the way I do,
When every thought leads back to you.
No message sent, no call, no sign,
But in my mind, you're always mine.
Though silence grows, and time moves on,
My heart still waits, though you're long gone.

In Every Tear

"Every tear I shed is tied to you. There's a strange comfort in remembering you, even if it brings pain. I think of all the times I wish I could have held on tighter, and all the things I left unsaid. Sometimes, crying is the only way to feel close to you, even if you're far away."

—-

I cry in quiet, no one sees,
The weight you left upon my knees.
Each tear that falls, I think of you,
A love that's lost, but always true.
The days are long, the nights are cold,
But in my heart, you're still a hold.
I wonder if you feel the same,
Or if I've lost this endless game.
In every tear, you live once more,
A ghost of love that I adore.
And though you're gone, and we're apart,
You still remain within my heart.

The Last Goodnight

"Every night, before I close my eyes, I think about you. There's an emptiness because I no longer hear your 'goodnight.' It's strange how something as simple as a small message made everything feel okay. Now, the silence feels heavier, and I wish I could go back to those nights where everything felt normal between us."

—-

I miss the way you'd say goodnight,
Your words would make the darkness light.
But now the silence fills the space,
No message left, no warm embrace.
The nights are long, and sleep won't stay,
Without your voice to guide the way.
I scroll through texts from days before,
When 'goodnight' wasn't such a chore.
But now I say it to the air,
Hoping somehow you'll feel it there.
Though miles apart and worlds away,
In my heart, you'll always stay.

Faded Conversations

"I go through our old conversations and smile at how simple things used to be. Every word, every reply felt like a connection. But now those words feel faded, like they've lost meaning over time. I wonder if you go back to those chats, too, or if they're just memories left behind for me to hold onto alone."

—-

I read our chats from days gone by,
And wonder if you even try
To think of me, like I do you,
In every word, our story grew.
But now those words feel so far gone,
Like faded ink, they don't stay long.
I search for meaning in each line,
But all I find is empty time.
I wonder if you feel the same,
Or if our talk was just a game.
Still, I read those words once more,
Hoping they'll mean what they did before.

Lost in Your Silence

"Every time I see your name on my phone, I pause, hoping for a message, a call, anything. But it never comes. Your silence is louder than words, and it hurts more than I can explain. I wonder if you ever think of me, the way I think of you, or if you've moved on completely. Even though I know I shouldn't, I still wait for something—anything—from you."

—

I wait for words that never come,
A simple call, but you send none.
Your silence wraps around my mind,
A louder sound I cannot find.
I scroll your name, just to feel,
A glimpse of you that still feels real.
But nothing breaks this heavy spell,
In your silence, I dwell and dwell.
I wonder if you think of me,
Or if I'm just a memory.
Still, I wait, though I know it's wrong,
In your silence, I've stayed too long.

The Night We Never Spoke

"Sometimes I lie awake, thinking about all the things I never said to you. I replay conversations in my head, imagining how things could have gone differently. There are so many moments I wish I could take back, and so many words I wish I could say now. But every night ends the same way—with me lying there, in silence, thinking of you."

—-

I lie awake, the night so still,
With words unspoken that could fill
The space between us, far and wide,
The things I wish I'd never hide.
I think of times we used to share,
When every thought, you seemed to care.
But now those moments slip away,
And words I kept now lose their way.
The night we never spoke feels long,
A quiet hurt that feels so wrong.
But still, I lie here, wide awake,
Wishing for words we didn't make.

Echoes of the Past

"Every corner of my life still holds echoes of our past moments. From the places we used to visit to the little things we used to do together, everything reminds me of you. Even though we're no longer in each other's lives, these echoes make it hard to move on. I find myself revisiting those memories, hoping to relive the happiness we once shared."

—-

In every street we used to roam,
I see reminders of our home.
The places where we laughed and talked,
Now hold memories where I've walked.
The café where we sipped our tea,
Now just a spot where I feel the sea
Of nostalgia and forgotten grace,
A silent echo of your face.
I pass by old familiar sights,
And in the shadows of the nights,
I find your laughter in the air,
Though you're no longer anywhere.

The Unwritten Letters

"I often imagine writing you letters that I never send. Each letter would hold my deepest feelings and thoughts, things I could never express to you directly. These unwritten letters are a way for me to channel my emotions, even if they remain unsent. They capture everything I wish I could say, but never will."

—-

I draft the words I'd never send,
In letters that I never pen.
Each line holds what I feel inside,
But only my heart will ever confide.
I write of dreams we never shared,
Of hopes and fears, of how I cared.
These pages hold my silent cries,
Of love unspoken, deep goodbyes.
I fold each letter, place it away,
A testament to what I can't say.
Though you'll never read a line,
In these unwritten notes, you're mine.

The Spaces You Left

"Your absence has created empty spaces in my life that I can't seem to fill. From the spot on the sofa where you used to sit to the places where we shared our conversations, everything feels incomplete without you. These empty spaces are constant reminders of what once was and what could have been."

—

In the corner of my quiet room,
Your absence casts a subtle gloom.
The spot you left now feels so bare,
A vacant place where you once were there.
The sofa where we used to sit,
Holds echoes of our laughter fit.
The table where we shared our meals,
Now just a space where silence heals.
I trace the spots where you once stood,
In every corner, I find no good.
The empty spaces tell a tale,
Of love that's lost, but still prevails.

The Forgotten Songs

"Songs that once meant everything to us now only serve as reminders of our past. Each melody brings back memories of the times we spent together. Though these songs are beautiful, they've become bittersweet because they echo moments I can no longer experience with you."

The songs we played in days of old,
Now play a tune that's harsh and cold.
Each melody that we once knew,
Now sings a song of missing you.
The notes we danced to in the night,
Are now just echoes in the light.
The lyrics that once felt so true,
Now seem to mourn what we went through.
I hear the music, feel the strain,
Of memories that bring me pain.
Yet still, these songs I play on repeat,
A bittersweet, familiar beat.

The Forgotten Spaces

"Certain places that used to be special to us now only bring a sense of loss. Whether it's the park where we used to walk or the café where we had our conversations, these places have become reminders of what was once a cherished part of my life. They're now empty spaces filled with memories and longing."

—-

The park where we would stroll and dream,
Now feels empty, lost its gleam.
The benches where we used to rest,
Are just cold seats, now not blessed.
The café where our laughter rang,
Is silent now, no joy it sang.
The tables where we shared our time,
Now hold the echoes of a rhyme.
These spaces once were filled with light,
Now carry shadows of our night.
The places where our hearts once soared,
Now leave me longing, feeling bored.

The Unspoken Words

"There are so many things I wished I could have told you, but the words never came out. Each moment we spent together was filled with unspoken sentiments. Now, those words linger in my mind, never expressed, and they leave me with a bittersweet feeling of what might have been."

—-

There were words I never spoke,
In every pause, in every joke.
The things I wanted you to hear,
Are now just echoes, far and near.
The moments where I held my tongue,
Are now the songs that go unsung.
The feelings that I kept inside,
Are buried deep, where dreams reside.
I think of all I wished to say,
But silence kept them far away.
In every unspoken word,
A love that's lost, but still inferred.

The Echo of Empty Spaces

"Certain places that we used to visit together now feel hollow without you. Whether it's the park bench where we sat or the café corner where we talked, these spaces seem to echo with the memories of our time together. They remind me of the joy we once shared and the emptiness I feel now."

—-

The park bench where we used to meet,
Now feels so cold beneath my feet.
The space you filled is now a void,
A silent echo, now destroyed.
The café corner where we laughed,
Now holds a past that's long since passed.
The chairs we sat in, side by side,
Are just empty seats where memories hide.
These empty spaces tell a tale,
Of love that once was, now frail.
In every corner, I still seek,
The joy that once was, now so meek.

The Unsent Messages

"I often find myself typing messages to you that I never send. Each unsent message holds my deepest feelings and thoughts. It's a way for me to express what I can't say directly, capturing all the emotions I wish I could share with you."

—-

I type the words I'll never send,
A message to a distant friend.
Each line holds what I long to say,
But stays unsent, just fades away.
The words I draft, the thoughts I share,
Are left alone in silent air.
No "send" button pressed, no voice to hear,
Just written words that hold my fear.
I wish that you could read each line,
To understand this heart of mine.
But for now, these messages remain,
Unsent, unseen, a silent pain.

The Empty Chair

"Sometimes I find myself sitting in the places we used to be together, and the absence of you feels palpable. An empty chair at the table or a vacant spot on the couch makes me acutely aware of your absence. It's a stark reminder of how much I miss the moments we shared."

—

The empty chair where you would sit,
Now feels so cold, a perfect fit
For the void you left behind,
A space that echoes in my mind.
The table where we used to dine,
Now just holds a single line.
Your absence fills the space so wide,
A reminder of our time denied.
I look at places once so bright,
Now filled with shadows of the night.
The empty chair, the vacant spot,
Are memories that sting a lot.

The Fading Pictures

"Photos of us together used to bring joy, but now they serve as reminders of what we've lost. As time passes, these pictures start to fade, both literally and emotionally. They capture moments of happiness that now feel distant and out of reach."

—-

The pictures on the wall are blurred,
With memories that now seem stirred.
The smiles we shared, the times we had,
Are fading now, both good and bad.
The frames are dusty, edges worn,
Each photo tells of love forlorn.
The colors fade, the smiles dim,
A testament to what's grown slim.
I look at these with a wistful sigh,
At moments that have passed me by.
The fading pictures tell a tale,
Of love that's lost, but still prevails.

The Unused Gifts

"Sometimes I think about the gifts I bought for you, which now remain unused. Each one was chosen with care and love, hoping to express my feelings. Now, they sit untouched, a reminder of what I wanted to give you and the emotions I hoped to share."

—-

The gifts I bought with all my heart,
Now lie untouched, a work of art.
Each one meant to show my care,
But now they rest, alone, laid bare.
The trinkets, tokens, and the notes,
Are like lost dreams on drifting boats.
They wait for you, but never find,
A place to rest, a love aligned.
These unused gifts are silent cries,
Of feelings that I can't disguise.
Each one a piece of my soul's desire,
Now unclaimed, lost in the mire.

The Silent Calls

"I often pick up my phone, thinking about calling you, but then I hesitate and put it down. Each missed call represents a moment when I wanted to reach out, but couldn't. The silence on the other end becomes a painful reminder of our separation."

—-

I reach for my phone, and dial your name,
But silence answers, much the same.
Each call I make, but never send,
Holds all the words I wish to blend.
The voicemail waits, the line stays clear,
A silent space where you're not near.
Each ring I hear is just a sound,
Of feelings lost, but still profound.
The calls remain in moments lost,
A painful echo, at what cost?
I pick up my phone, then let it be,
In silent calls, you're here with me.

The Forgotten Smiles

"Once, your smile was the brightest part of my day, a beacon of warmth and joy. Now, those smiles are just memories, and they seem to fade as time passes. Each smile captured in my mind is a reminder of the happiness we shared and the emptiness left behind."

—

Your smile used to light the day,
A warmth that chased my fears away.
But now those smiles are just a blur,
A fading light, a memory's stir.
The laughter that we used to share,
Now echoes in the empty air.
Your smile, once bright, now feels so dim,
A distant star, a faded hymn.
I reach for moments filled with cheer,
But they dissolve, and you're not here.
The forgotten smiles are all I keep,
In dreams where memories softly seep.

The Unanswered Questions

"There are so many things I wish I could ask you, but I know I'll never get answers. Each question is a piece of my heart, left hanging in the air. These unanswered questions keep me wondering about what might have been and why things turned out the way they did."

I have questions left unasked,
In every moment, you were masked.
The things I wonder, the doubts I keep,
Are left unanswered, buried deep.
Why did we drift, why did we part?
These questions weigh heavy on my heart.
I ponder what you might have said,
But silence answers instead.
The queries linger, never clear,
In dreams where you are still near.
The unanswered questions haunt my mind,
In the echoes of a love left behind.

The Empty Calendar

"Each day on the calendar used to be marked with moments we shared. Now, as I look at the empty squares, I am reminded of the days that could have been filled with our memories. The empty calendar reflects the absence of you and the days that now feel hollow without you."

—-

The calendar hangs, empty and stark,
Once filled with days that left a mark.
The dates we'd planned, now left behind,
Are silent pages, intertwined.
The days we hoped to share are gone,
Replaced by moments I dwell upon.
Each blank square is a silent plea,
For the time we lost, now left to be.
The empty dates, the void they show,
Are reminders of the love I know.
In each blank space, your absence shows,
A testament to what I chose.

The Unread Messages

"There are messages I wrote for you but never sent, filled with the thoughts and emotions I couldn't express. These messages remain unread, a collection of my heart's secrets and feelings that never found their way to you. They are a silent testament to my unspoken words."

—-

The messages I wrote, but never sent,
Hold all the feelings I never spent.
Each word, each line, a secret kept,
In drafts of love where dreams have slept.
The inbox remains, untouched and still,
A place where my heart's thoughts fulfill.
The messages stay in a quiet haze,
A collection of unspoken praise.
Unread, they sit in silent grace,
A testament to love's embrace.
In every draft, my heart's true plea,
A love that's lost, yet still to be.

The Forgotten Playlist

"Music that once played a significant role in our time together now feels bittersweet. The playlist of songs we used to enjoy has become a reminder of the moments we shared. Each song brings back memories of you, but also highlights the emptiness left in your absence."

—-

The playlist that we once would play,
Now echoes memories of yesterday.
The songs we danced to, laughed, and cried,
Now stir a heart where dreams have died.
The melodies that filled our space,
Now play a tune I can't replace.
Each note a whisper of our past,
In every song, a shadow cast.
I listen, but the joy has waned,
The music's touch now feels so strained.
The forgotten playlist, once so dear,
Now sings a song of loss and fear.

The Missed Moments

"There were countless moments I wished we could have shared, but they slipped away. Each missed opportunity to talk, to laugh, or to simply be together now feels like a gap in my life. These missed moments are reminders of what could have been, leaving a lingering sense of regret."

—-

The moments that we could not seize,
Are like a breeze that leaves with ease.
The times we missed, the words unspoken,
Are memories that leave me broken.
The laughter that we never shared,
The times I wished that you had cared.
Each missed chance, a silent plea,
For moments lost that could have been.
I think of what we might have done,
The times we lost beneath the sun.
The missed moments, like fleeting dreams,
Are echoes of unspoken themes.

The Abandoned Notes

"Sometimes I would jot down thoughts and feelings I wanted to share with you, but they remain abandoned in my notebooks. These notes are filled with unspoken emotions and unsent messages, now just reminders of my heart's unfulfilled desires."

—-

The notes I wrote with trembling hand,
Now lie forgotten in the sand.
Each page a whisper of my soul,
A tale of love that took its toll.
The words I penned but never gave,
Are left alone, a silent grave.
The thoughts I had, the dreams I spun,
Now sit in silence, one by one.
The abandoned notes are lost and bare,
A testament to love and care.
In every line, my heart's true plea,
A love that's lost but still to be.

The Faded Dreams

"Dreams we once shared about our future now seem distant and faded. What we envisioned together has become a blur, replaced by reality that falls short. These faded dreams are a painful reminder of the future that could have been."

—-

The dreams we spun in twilight's grace,
Now fade away, without a trace.
The future we imagined bright,
Now blurs with shadows in the night.
The plans we made, the paths we drew,
Are now just echoes of what's true.
The visions once so clear and near,
Now distant dreams that disappear.
In every thought of what could be,
The faded dreams still call to me.
They linger on in quiet sighs,
A love that's lost beneath the skies.

The Empty Message Drafts

"There are countless drafts of messages I started to write for you but never sent. Each draft holds my heartfelt thoughts and wishes, but they remain unsent and unspoken. These empty drafts symbolize the words I couldn't share and the emotions that never reached you."

—-

In drafts of messages, I write,
Words meant for you, but out of sight.
Each line a whisper of my heart,
Yet left unsent, a work of art.
The drafts remain in silence still,
A testament to unspoken will.
Each message crafted, never sent,
Holds dreams and thoughts I never meant.
The empty drafts are all I keep,
A secret trove of feelings deep.
In every word that's left unshared,
Lies love that's lost, but always cared.

The Forgotten Places

"Places we used to visit together now feel deserted and forlorn. Each location that once held special memories now stands empty and cold. These forgotten places are reminders of the joy we once shared and the emptiness that has followed."

—-

The places where we used to roam,
Now feel like shadows of our home.
The paths we walked, now worn and cold,
Are memories of stories told.
The parks, the streets, the spots we knew,
Are now just spaces, feeling blue.
The laughter that we once did share,
Is now a ghost in the empty air.
These forgotten places hold our past,
A silent echo that won't last.
In every corner, I still seek,
The joy we had, now feeling weak.

The Photo Frames

"Photos of us that used to bring joy now serve as painful reminders. Each picture on the wall or in my phone is a snapshot of happier times. I keep looking at them, hoping to relive those moments, but they only highlight how things have changed."

The photo frames that line the wall,
Now hold memories, but feel so small.
Each image once a cherished sight,
Now just a ghost of what felt right.
I trace your smile in every shot,
Recalling moments, now forgot.
The photos bring both joy and pain,
A visual song in a silent refrain.
I stare at these with longing eyes,
At frozen times that no longer rise.
The photo frames, once filled with cheer,
Now hold the echoes of a love sincere.

The Imagined Encounters

"I often daydream about meeting you, imagining scenarios where we reconnect. These daydreams are filled with conversations and moments we never had. Each imagined encounter is a bittersweet escape from reality, where everything turns out perfectly."

—-

In daydreams, I imagine where we meet,
In places warm and moments sweet.
We talk and laugh, we walk anew,
In dreams where all my hopes come true.
I picture us in every scene,
In conversations, calm and serene.
The moments we could never share,
Are painted vivid in the air.
These imagined encounters are my reprieve,
From a reality where I grieve.
In dreams, our paths are intertwined,
In daydreams where your love I find.

The Songs of Us

"Songs that once played in our shared moments now seem to speak directly to my feelings. I listen to these melodies and find myself relating every lyric to our relationship. Each song becomes a poignant reminder of the love I hold."

—-

The songs that played when we were near,
Now echo softly, loud and clear.
Each lyric seems to speak of us,
In melodies that gently fuss.
I hear the tunes and feel your touch,
In every note, I miss so much.
The songs, once ours, now feel so true,
A serenade of me and you.
These melodies are bittersweet,
In every chord, our hearts could meet.
The songs remind me of the past,
In every verse, a love that lasts.

The Untouched Letters

"I write letters to you that I'll never send, pouring out my deepest feelings. These letters remain untouched and unread, a private collection of my emotions. They are a testament to the love I feel, even though they'll never reach you."

—-

The letters that I write with care,
Are left alone in silent air.
Each word a piece of my heart's plea,
Untouched, unseen, and never free.
I pen my feelings, raw and true,
In pages meant to reach you.
But these letters lie without a sound,
In a place where love's not found.
They are a testament to my soul,
A story of a love untold.
In every line, my heart's lament,
In letters never sent, but meant.

The Midnight Thoughts

"At night, when the world is quiet, my thoughts often drift to you. In the stillness, I replay our memories and imagine conversations we never had. These midnight thoughts are a blend of longing and reflection, where my emotions run deep."

—-

In the quiet of the midnight hour,
My thoughts of you hold such power.
The stillness brings your name to light,
In dreams where you feel close at night.
I replay moments, soft and sweet,
In the silence where our hearts could meet.
Conversations we never had,
Are vivid dreams that make me sad.
The midnight thoughts, they weave and wind,
In echoes of a love I find.
In every quiet, peaceful sigh,
You are the moon that lights my sky.

The Forgotten Letters

"Old letters and messages, once meant to be shared, now remain forgotten. Each one is a piece of my heart that never made it to you. They symbolize my unspoken feelings and the dreams I had for us."

—-

The letters that I wrote in vain,
Are tucked away in memory's chain.
Each page a glimpse of what I felt,
In words that time and silence dealt.
They lay forgotten, sealed and still,
A testament to love's lost will.
The letters that were never sent,
Hold dreams and hopes that came and went.
In each forgotten, dusty pile,
Lies a heart that waits awhile.
The letters are my silent plea,
To the love that's never meant for me.

The Echoes of Laughter

"Moments of laughter we shared are now just echoes in my mind. I often find myself recalling those times, wishing I could relive them. These echoes are bittersweet reminders of a time when everything seemed perfect."

—-

The laughter that we used to share,
Now echoes softly in the air.
The joy we had, now feels so far,
A distant memory, a fading star.
I hear the echoes of our cheer,
In moments that are now unclear.
The sounds of laughter, light and free,
Are now just whispers left to be.
In every laugh that used to ring,
Lies a heartache that I can't bring.
The echoes of a time we knew,
Are gentle reminders of the love I rue.

The Dreamt Conversations

"I often imagine conversations with you that never happened. These dreamt dialogues are filled with the things I wish I could say and hear. They are a way for me to feel close to you, even though these exchanges remain in my mind."

—-

In dreams, I talk to you so clear,
In conversations we never steer.
The words I long to say, to hear,
Are echoes in my mind, sincere.
I imagine dialogues we'd share,
In moments when you'd truly care.
The conversations that could have been,
Are dreamt exchanges, soft and keen.
These dreamt talks are where you stay,
In whispered words that fade away.
In every chat I wish I had,
Lies the love that makes me sad.

The Unsent Gifts

"Over time, I've gathered gifts I wanted to give you but never did. Each gift represents my affection and the moments I wished to share. They remain untouched, a reminder of my unfulfilled intentions and the love I still hold."

—-

The gifts I bought, wrapped with care,
Are left alone, a silent prayer.
Each token of my love for you,
Now waits in shadows, cold and blue.
The presents that I planned to give,
Are buried in a dream I live.
Each one a symbol of my heart,
Now sits in stillness, torn apart.
These unsent gifts are dreams deferred,
In every ribbon, my heart is stirred.
A love that's left without its chance,
In every gift, a mournful glance.

The Replayed Memories

"Certain memories with you replay in my mind like old films. I revisit them repeatedly, cherishing the good times while grappling with their loss. These memories are a mix of comfort and sorrow, constantly replayed in the theater of my heart."

—-

The memories replay, soft and clear,
In the theater of my mind, dear.
Scenes of us that play on loop,
In dreams where joy and sorrow stoop.
I watch the moments that we had,
In memories both sweet and sad.
The times we shared are films in flight,
In my heart's endless, quiet night.
These replayed scenes are bittersweet,
In every frame, our hearts could meet.
The memories, both bright and dim,
Are echoes of a love too grim.

The Silent Messages

"I compose messages in my mind, wanting to reach out to you, but they remain unsent. These silent messages are filled with my deepest feelings and thoughts, never delivered but always felt. They represent my longing and the words I wish I could say."

—-

The messages I write in vain,
Remain unsent, a silent strain.
Each word a piece of what I feel,
In letters that will never heal.
I draft my thoughts and dreams for you,
In messages that are left untrue.
The silence wraps them tight in fate,
A love unspoken, but innate.
These silent messages are my plea,
To the heart that will not see.
In every line and hidden sigh,
Lies a love that will not die.

The Echoes in the Dark

"In the quiet of night, I often hear echoes of our past conversations and moments. These echoes are vivid reminders of the connection we once had, now just shadows that linger in the dark. They are a haunting reminder of what used to be."

—-

The echoes in the dark still play,
Of conversations from yesterday.
In silence, I hear the words we said,
In shadows where our memories tread.
The echoes linger, soft and low,
In every whisper, our love's glow.
The dark holds fragments of our past,
In echoes that forever last.
These nightly echoes haunt my mind,
In every sound, our hearts unwind.
The darkness holds what we once knew,
In echoes of a love so true.

The Forgotten Promises

"I made promises to you that remain unfulfilled. These promises were expressions of my deep commitment and hopes for us, but they have faded away. Each forgotten promise is a reminder of my unwavering affection and the dreams that never came to pass."

—-

The promises I made to you,
Are left behind, no longer true.
Each vow a piece of what I planned,
Now scattered like the drifting sand.
The words I spoke with earnest heart,
Are memories that drift apart.
The promises, now lost in time,
Are echoes of a love's lost rhyme.
These forgotten vows are all I keep,
In dreams where promises still seep.
In every word, a love that yearns,
For promises that will not return.

The Unspoken Words

"Many things I wanted to say to you remain unsaid. These unspoken words carry my deepest emotions and thoughts that I never had the courage to voice. They linger in my heart, representing my love and the things I wish I could share with you."

The words I wanted to say to you,
Remain unsaid, hidden from view.
Each thought I kept within my heart,
Is a piece of love that set apart.
I crafted sentences in silent hope,
In dreams where we could surely cope.
The unspoken words are whispers faint,
In every silence, my heart's complaint.
These unsaid things are shadows cast,
In echoes of a love that's passed.
In every thought I wished to share,
Lies a love that's still laid bare.

The Unused Spaces

"There are places I reserved in my life for you, spaces that were meant for shared moments and memories. Now, these spaces remain empty, filled with the absence of you. They are silent reminders of the future that never was."

—-

The spaces in my heart were set,
For moments with you, I won't forget.
These places now lie bare and cold,
In the absence of the love I hold.
The seats we'd fill, the paths we'd walk,
Are empty now, without your talk.
The spaces that were once our own,
Are silent, empty, and alone.
These unused spaces mark the past,
In every corner, a love that's cast.
In every void and vacant place,
Lies a memory of your embrace.

The Daydreamed Conversations

"I often daydream about conversations we might have had. In my mind, I envision discussions full of laughter and intimacy. These daydreamed conversations are a way for me to feel close to you, even though they never happen in reality."

—-

In daydreams, I picture us in talk,
In places where we used to walk.
Our conversations flow so free,
In dreams where you are next to me.
I imagine laughter and sweet replies,
In scenes where love never dies.
The words we'd share, the jokes we'd make,
Are daydreams that my heart does take.
These imagined chats are bittersweet,
In every line, our hearts could meet.
The daydreams fill the empty space,
With echoes of your warm embrace.

The Abandoned Places

"Places where we spent time together now feel abandoned and forlorn. They serve as reminders of the joy we once shared, now replaced by solitude. These abandoned places are silent witnesses to the love that has faded."

—-

The places where we once would go,
Now stand abandoned, feeling low.
The benches, streets, and corners dear,
Are empty now, without your cheer.
These spots we cherished now lie still,
A quiet echo of the thrill.
The joy we had in these old haunts,
Is now a ghost that softly taunts.
The abandoned places hold our past,
In memories that did not last.
In every silent, vacant space,
Lies a love that leaves no trace.

The Echoing Lullabies

"Lullabies and songs that once were a comfort now seem to echo my feelings for you. Each melody reminds me of the love I have and the dreams that remain unfulfilled. These echoing lullabies are a soothing yet painful reminder of what could have been."

—-

The lullabies that softly play,
Now echo dreams of yesterday.
In every tune, I find your grace,
In melodies that time erased.
The songs we shared in tender nights,
Now echo softly, out of sight.
Each lullaby, a wistful tune,
That brings me close to you too soon.
These echoing songs are bittersweet,
In every note, our hearts could meet.
The melodies are soft and kind,
Yet leave a longing in my mind.

The Half-Filled Diary

"My diary holds countless entries dedicated to you, filled with thoughts and feelings I never shared. Each page is half-written, a testament to the love and emotions that remain unspoken. The diary stands as a silent keeper of my heart's secrets."

—-

In my diary, the pages wait,
Half-filled with dreams of our shared fate.
Each entry holds the words unspoken,
A love that time has left unbroken.
The lines are filled with hope and ache,
Of dreams we never got to make.
The diary, a silent keeper,
Of love that grows, yet grows deeper.
These half-written thoughts remain,
A testament to a silent pain.
In every page, my heart does yearn,
For the love that will not return.

The Unseen Stars

"Stars that once seemed bright now feel distant and out of reach. I once hoped they would shine on our shared dreams, but now they merely remind me of the space between us. They are a metaphor for the love I long for, yet can never grasp."

—-

The stars that sparkled in our skies,
Now seem distant, out of sight.
They once were guides for our shared dreams,
Now shadows of forgotten beams.
The night sky holds the love we knew,
In stars that now feel cold and blue.
The constellations, once so near,
Now echo dreams that disappear.
These unseen stars mark what was lost,
In every twinkle, a love crossed.
The night's vast sky holds space and time,
Where love remains a distant chime.

The Wandering Paths

"I often walk the paths we once shared, hoping to feel close to you. These paths now feel empty, with only memories as company. They are a reflection of my journey through love, where the destination remains out of reach."

—-

I wander paths where we once tread,
In search of memories we both shed.
The trails we walked are empty now,
With only echoes left to bow.
The streets and lanes we used to roam,
Are quiet now, no longer home.
I walk these paths to feel you near,
Yet find only shadows, lost and clear.
These wandering ways are bittersweet,
In every step, our hearts could meet.
The paths we shared now gently part,
Leaving traces in my heart.

The Unplayed Records

"Records of our favorite songs lie untouched, waiting to be played. Each one holds a memory of our time together, but remains silent. These unplayed records symbolize the moments that are frozen in time, waiting for a tune that will never come."

—

The records on the shelf stand still,
Untouched by time, a silent thrill.
Each song a memory we knew,
Now waits for notes that won't come through.
The melodies that once were ours,
Are quiet now, devoid of powers.
The records hold our songs so clear,
Yet silence is all I hear.
These unplayed tunes are bittersweet,
In every pause, our hearts could meet.
The silence holds our love's refrain,
In every track, a hidden pain.

The Fading Ink

"Letters and notes I wrote to you are slowly fading away, much like the memories of our time together. The fading ink symbolizes how the moments we shared are gradually disappearing from my life, leaving only traces of what once was."

—-

The ink on letters starts to fade,
Like memories that time has made.
Each note I penned with heartfelt care,
Now blurs with time, no longer there.
The words we shared are dimming fast,
In pages where our love did last.
The fading ink reflects the pain,
Of love that slips away again.
These fading letters hold our past,
In every blur, a love that's cast.
The ink may fade, but hearts remain,
In memories of a sweet refrain.

The Unanswered Calls

"My phone holds a record of calls I made to you that were never answered. Each missed call is a reminder of my longing and the conversations we never had. They symbolize my desire to reach out, even when you remain unreachable."

—-

The calls I made to you in vain,
Are echoes of my heart's refrain.
Each ring that met with silent tone,
Is a reminder of love unknown.
The missed calls mark my heartfelt plea,
To reach a love that's lost to me.
The phone holds records of my cries,
In every dial, my love's goodbyes.
These unanswered calls are bittersweet,
In every ring, our hearts could meet.
The silence on the other end,
Holds a love that cannot mend.

A Little Note :)

You might think that I don't remember you, right? But don't ever think that. Could I ever forget you? Could it even be possible? No.

From the moment I wake up to the moment I sleep, and throughout the day, it's always thoughts of you and memories of you. My heart desperately wants to message you, to ask how you're doing and how your day has been. I want to reach out so much, but I don't know why I hesitate. I worry that if I do message, you might think I'm bothering you. I'm unsure why these thoughts come to mind.

But one thing I'm certain of is that you probably don't remember me. Is that true :(?

About the Author

Mrigendra Bharti, born on June 29, 2004, in South Delhi, India, is a multifaceted individual recognized as the owner of Mrigendra Bharti Group InfoTech India Co. Pvt Ltd. Beyond his entrepreneurial endeavors, he is a distinguished music producer, director, and a budding writer.

Embarking on his professional journey at a young age, Mrigendra Bharti's visionary leadership has led to the establishment of several successful ventures, including Croma Music Series Entertainment, Sellbrochure, Fauget Innovative, and more.

What sets Mrigendra apart is his early initiation into the world of business. His foray into the unknown realms of entrepreneurship began during his 10th-grade years, where he delved into the music industry. This initial venture laid the foundation for subsequent achievements, showcasing his dedication and resilience.

Having honed his skills in music, Mrigendra Bharti not only demonstrated significant growth in his craft but also expanded his professional network. His passion extends beyond music, encompassing app and website development, as well as graphic design.

Fueled by his creative aspirations, Mrigendra established the Mrigendra Bharti Group, a company specializing in website and app development. Currently, he collaborates with a dedicated team, collectively working on ambitious projects that promise innovation and excellence.

Mrigendra's journey serves as an inspiration, particularly for today's students, highlighting the potential of youthful determination and the ability to transform innovative ideas into successful businesses. As he continues to make strides in various domains, Mrigendra Bharti remains a dynamic force, contributing vibrancy to the realms of business, music, and technology.

Read more at https://www.imwriter-mrigendra.rf.gd.